I0812531

History of the Titanic

People on the Titanic

by Julie Murray

2

Dash!
LEVELED READERS
An Imprint of Abdo Zoom • abdobooks.com

Dash!
LEVELED READERS

Level 1 – Beginning
Short and simple sentences with familiar words or patterns for children who are beginning to understand how letters and sounds go together.

Level 2 – Emerging
Longer words and sentences with more complex language patterns for readers who are practicing common words and letter sounds.

Level 3 – Transitional
More developed language and vocabulary for readers who are becoming more independent.

THIS BOOK CONTAINS RECYCLED MATERIALS

abdobooks.com

Published by Abdo Zoom, a division of ABDO, PO Box 398166, Minneapolis, Minnesota 55439.
Copyright © 2025 by Abdo Consulting Group, Inc. International copyrights reserved in all countries. No part of this book may be reproduced in any form without written permission from the publisher.
Dash!™ is a trademark and logo of Abdo Zoom.

Printed in the United States of America, North Mankato, Minnesota.
102024
012025

Photo Credits: Getty Images, Shutterstock
Production Contributors: Kenny Abdo, Jennie Forsberg, Grace Hansen, John Hansen
Design Contributors: Candice Keimig, Neil Klinepier

Library of Congress Control Number: 2024936554

Publisher's Cataloging in Publication Data

Names: Murray, Julie, author.
Title: People on the Titanic / by Julie Murray
Description: Minneapolis, Minnesota : Abdo Zoom, 2025 | Series: History of the Titanic | Includes online resources and index.
Identifiers: ISBN 9781098287269 (lib. bdg.) | ISBN 9781098287962 (ebook) | ISBN 9781098288310 (Read-to-me ebook)
Subjects: LCSH: Ships--Passenger lists--Juvenile literature. | Passenger ships--Juvenile literature. | Shipwrecks--North Atlantic Ocean--Juvenile literature. | Historic ships--Juvenile literature. | Titanic (Steamship)--Juvenile literature.
Classification: DDC 910.9163--dc23

Table of Contents

People on the *Titanic*

The **RMS** *Titanic* set sail from Southampton, England, on April 10, 1912, with 2,240 passengers and crew onboard.

The passengers were from many different backgrounds. Their experiences on the ship were different too.

The richest people were in first class. First-class passengers mainly included business owners and their wives. They slept in private **suites**.

The first-class area had a grand dining room. It also had a swimming pool and gym.

12

Second-class passengers slept in shared **cabins**. Many were teachers and writers.

Third-class passengers were mainly **immigrants**. Their **cabins** could have up to 10 beds.

Notable Passengers

Edward John Smith was the captain of the **RMS** *Titanic*. He went down with the ship.

The "Unsinkable Molly Brown" was a survivor. She helped passengers escape the ship and urged people to rescue those who had gone into the water.

19

Millvina Dean was the last living *Titanic* survivor. She died in 2009 at 97 years old.

More Facts

- The *Titanic's* destination was New York City.

- More than 1,500 people died in the sinking of the *Titanic*. Only 340 bodies were recovered.

- There were 706 survivors, meaning that just 31.6% of the people onboard the ship lived.

Glossary

cabin - a room or compartment in a ship or airplane.

immigrant - a person who moves permanently to another country from his or her native land.

RMS - short for Royal Mail Ship.

suite - several rooms that are connected.

Index

Online Resources

Booklinks
NONFICTION NETWORK
FREE! ONLINE NONFICTION RESOURCES

To learn more about people on the *Titanic*, please visit **abdobooklinks.com** or scan this QR code. These links are routinely monitored and updated to provide the most current information available.